# OMG!

## PRAYERS FOR TEENAGERS BY TEENAGERS

MARTHA DOMMETT
ELEANOR HERBERT

KEVIN MAYHEW LTD

First published in 2020 by Kevin Mayhew Ltd,
Rattlesden,
Stowmarket,
Suffolk, IP14 3BW
www.kevinmayhew.com



ISBN (paperback) 978-1-8385-8092-6
ISBN (eBook) 978-1-8385-8093-3
Paperback product code 1501672
eBook product code 1501673



Created with Vellum

# OMG!
Prayers for Teenagers *by* Teenagers

CONTENTS

# Introduction

# TEENAGERS . . .

As teenagers, we go through A LOT! Our teen years are really exciting, but full of change and this can be hard to navigate. Amazingly we don't have to do this on our own. God is always there to guide and protect us. All we need to do is ask for his help... and we can do this through prayer.

Prayer is just us chatting to God, honestly and openly. We don't have to use big words or fancy names. However, when we are experiencing something we are struggling to understand, it can be hard to know what to pray or to remember things to still be thankful for.

This book is designed to help shape these conversations with God and facilitate a space where it can be just us and him, with no distractions. Both teenagers ourselves, but at quite different stages of life from one another, we have drawn on our own stories, as well as significant themes, identified by a wider group of young people, to ensure our prayers are useful and relatable. For each theme there are two prayers, one shorter and one longer, as well as relevant bible verses.

Being a teenager is busy. You have school, homework, as

well as other commitments and you want to spend your free time doing things you enjoy, like hanging out with mates, so it can be hard to make time for God. We encourage you to use these prayers in any way that works for you. Feel free to adapt them to make them more personal. We pray this book enables you to talk to God even when you can't quite seem to find the words.

Most of all, we pray you will enjoy seeing all the incredible things God can do in your life!

# Prayers

# 1 ANGER

. . . be quick to listen, slow to speak, slow to anger; for your anger does not produce God's righteousness.

James 1:19-21

*I'm feeling so angry, God,*
*like I'm going to explode!*

*I have been suppressing this for a while*
*and now it is fizzing and heavy.*

*It has been building up and up*
*and I can't hold it for any longer*
*and I raise it to you now.*

*I pray you will lift it all away from me and*
*overflow my heart with your love*
*and a forgiving spirit.*

*Use these feelings to fuel my passion*
*for justice*
*and for unity.*

*Amen*

---

*Lord, I'm angry!*
*Angry at everyone around me,*
*angry at the way things have turned out,*
*angry at myself,*
*my body,*
*angry at even the smallest things.*

*Why are people sometimes so, so annoying?*
*I'm kind to them yet they can be so mean*
*to me.*
*Nothing feels fair.*

*It feels like tiny thoughts*
*that slipped through my mind*
*have come up again,*
*but this time they are making me so angry.*

*Everything has just built up inside of me*
*and I just want to scream*
*until it goes away.*

*I want to shout.*
*I want to cry.*
*I want to break something!*

*I want all the people who have done wrong*
*to see their mistake.*
*I feel so full of hate.*

*God,*
*you see all my thoughts,*
*you know why I'm feeling like this,*
*you heard all the words*
*that shouldn't have been said,*
*saw the situations*
*that brought me anger.*
*You know everything so well.*
*You know it all.*
*You know, Lord.*

*God,*
*I'm sorry for when I've done things I*
*shouldn't.*
*Lord take the weight off.*
*God, take it away from me.*
*Bring me peace Lord.*

*Amen*

# 2 ANXIETY

Cast all your anxiety on him, because he cares for you.

1 Peter 5:7

*God, I feel anxious all of the time.*
*When I am facing something new*
*or challenging,*
*my instinct is to immediately worry*
*about everything*
*that could go wrong.*

*I get a horrible feeling in my gut*
*which never goes away,*
*no matter what I do.*
*I feel overwhelmed*

*and on-edge.*
*I can't eat or sleep.*
*It prevents me from trying new things*
*because I can't stand*
*feeling like this*
*beforehand.*

*I pray you will overflow me*
*with your peace and Holy Spirit,*
*clearing out all of my fears*
*and negativity.*

*Reassure me, Lord.*
*Help me to remember*
*all of the times when I have felt like this in*
*my life*
*and then I ended up having*
*the best time ever!*
*I want my immediate feeling in situations*
*to be excitement,*
*not anxiety.*

*Give me the self-confidence and courage*
*I need*
*to continue stepping out of my comfort-zone.*
*Thank you that you are always with me, God,*
*and I have no reason*
*to be afraid.*

*Amen*

*Father,*
*I'm worried, stressed.*
*Things feel out of my control.*
*I feel like everything has been put on me.*
*I can't enjoy the moment.*

*Lord,*
*the Bible says to give all my troubles to you,*
*but honestly . . .*
*that doesn't leave me feeling completely calm.*
*I just keep feeling like I should have said this,*
*should have done that.*
*I keep overthinking everything.*

*Lord,*
*please answer my prayers,*
*walk alongside me,*
*help me to know your presence,*
*give me courage*
*to trust in you.*

*God,*
*please bring me peace.*

*Amen.*

# 3 BODY IMAGE

Or do you not know that your body is a temple of the Holy Spirit within you, which you have from God. 1 Corinthians 6:19

*Lord,*
*I'm not just my body,*
*but that's all I can think about,*
*my size and shape.*

*God,*
*I don't want to value my body over my being anymore.*
*I'm not just my face.*
*But that's all I can think about!*
*Why don't I look like the people I see on TV or in magazines?*
*I want to enjoy the way I look*

*and to stop feeling ashamed of it.*

*I'm not just my scars and marks.*
*But they're all I can think about.*
*I wish I had flawless skin.*
*God, I don't want to stay covered and hidden*
*forever!*
*Give me the self-esteem to love myself*
*completely and unconditionally,*
*just as you do.*

*Amen*

---

*Lord,*
*There is so much love on social media.*
*So much confidence, celebrating bodies.*
*So much empowerment.*
*But I also see so many photos of women in*
*bikinis,*
*perfect legs with a thigh gap,*
*perfect hair, perfect skin, a flat stomach.*
*And it's not just online,*
*but also on tv, bin magazines,*
*pictures of models in shops.*

*I don't know,*
*it just feels like once I look a certain way,*
*then I will be able to celebrate my body.*
*I feel like once I have that body,*
*everything else in life will just fall into place.*

*God, I know you love me*
*whatever I look like,*
*but that doesn't mean*
*the world will except me.*

*God, why did you give me this body?*
*Why God?*
*Why can't I look like them?*
*Why am I not good enough?*

*God, I want to love myself.*
*I want to feel happy in my body,*
*I want to be healthy.*
*I want to put you first, God,*
*but I'm struggling to not put a perfect body first.*
*I'm willing to do whatever it takes.*
*This makes me question how strong my faith is.*
*Why can't I just be one of those people who has a strong faith,*
*looks beautiful,*
*super confident*
*and their life just falls together?*

*I feel so fed up with my body.*
*I'm told that I'm your masterpiece,*
*your work of art,*
*but it's hard to really believe.*
*It doesn't just take away any negative feelings about my body.*

*God,*
*please help me to begin to see myself*
*the way you see me.*
*Guard me from comparing myself to someone else*
*every time I see a photo of an 'ideal' body.*
*Help me to appreciate*
*the amazing things*
*my body can do,*
*and my own beauty.*

*Amen*

# 4 BROKENNESS

---

The Lord is near to the brokenhearted, and saves the crushed in spirit.

Psalm 34:18

---

*Holy Spirit, come.*
*Find me here in my brokenness.*
*I feel like if I do anything else,*
*even just move,*
*I will completely crumble*
*and so I present every single shard of hurt*
*and pain*
*I am feeling right now*
*to you, God.*

*I feel bruised and betrayed*
*and I can't help but blame myself.*

*I need to know that I won't always feel like*
*this,*
*that I will be whole again.*
*Piece me back together*
*and fill me with your Spirit of love*
*and peace.*
*I pray you will guard and protect me,*
*holding my hand as I take my next step*
*and placing my feet*
*on solid ground.*
*I want to feel loved and free of this burden.*
*I lift it all to you now God.*

*Amen.*

---

*Lord,*
*things have been so hard.*
*It feels like things can't be the same again.*

*Lord,*
*I feel so trampled on,*
*so worthless,*
*so broken.*

*Lord, are you there?*
*Where have you been?*
*Why did you let me suffer?*
*I want things to change.*
*Please Lord,*
*bring me peace.*

*You cried with me,*
*suffered with me,*
*felt my pain.*
*You know me better than anyone else.*
*You know how to bring me joy.*

*Please Lord,*
*carry me through.*
*You can see what I can't,*
*so help me to trust in you.*

*Lord,*
*I bring you all my scars from the past.*
*Please take them.*
*Heal me,*
*save me Lord.*
*Help me to enjoy the little things.*
*Thank you for all you have done for me.*

*Lord,*
*help me to keep my focus on you,*
*and not to rely on the world*
*for happiness.*
*When things around me pull me down*
*and I begin to let myself get drawn into it,*
*help me to look to you to lift me up.*

*God,*
*I trust you will make things better.*
*I will trust that there is more goodness to come.*
*I will trust in your plan, Lord.*

*I will look forward to you revealing it to me*
*even though, right now,*
*it's really hard to imagine that things will*
*turn out okay.*

*Lord,*
*take my brokenness,*
*mend it,*
*make me even stronger*
*than I was before.*

*Amen.*

# 5 BULLYING

---

Be strong and bold; have no fear or dread of them, because it is the Lord your God who goes with you; he will not fail you or forsake you.

Deuteronomy 31:6

---

*Hey, God!*
*As you know,*
*some people are giving me a really hard time*
*at the moment*
*and I just can't take it anymore.*
*It is wearing me down and I feel exhausted by*
*it all.*
*Make it stop.*
*Surround me with people*
*who I can trust and confide in.*
*Shelter and protect me.*
*Give me the confidence*

*to stand up for myself*
*and clothe me in your strength*
*and peace.*

*I pray that you'll speak into the lives of those*
*who are bullying me*
*and show them your love*
*and your forgiveness.*

*Amen*

---

*God, Father, protect me.*
*The best part of my day*
*is going to sleep,*
*knowing the day is over,*
*but even then*
*I'm anxious.*

*How can I get up each morning*
*and find the strength*
*to face the day?*

*What's the point?*
*Where is my life going?*

*They crush my spirit, Lord.*
*I'm so self conscious,*
*so paranoid,*
*all the time.*

*I can't see my purpose.*
*Why am I like this?*
*Is it me?*
*Is it my fault?*
*Or is it them?*
*Surely nothing can be that bad in their lives*
*to do things like that to me.*

*Maybe one day they will realise.*
*I feel can't tell anyone either.*
*That will make it worse.*
*I'm trapped.*
*There is no way out, Lord.*

*Please, God,*
*you hear my cry!*
*Why hasn't it stopped?*

*Please, God, protect me.*
*Please, Father,*
*love me,*
*accept me,*
*know me,*
*know it all.*

*Please God,*
*save me,*
*shelter me.*
*I need you.*
*I need things to change.*

*Amen*

# 6 CALLING

I have called you by name, you are mine.
Isaiah 43:1

*What is my calling, God?*
*It's a question that I've been thinking about*
*for a while,*
*but I just can't seem to answer.*
*I know that you have given me so many*
*amazing gifts,*
*yet I don't know how to use these*
*to serve you.*

*Talk to me, Lord.*
*I want to hear the ways I can live my life*
*for you.*
*Sometimes,*
*I get confused*

*whether something is just what I want*
*or if it is from you, Lord.*

*Widen my eyes to the ways in which you*
*call me.*
*I pray you will help me*
*to listen tentatively*
*and to use my gifts*
*in any way I can.*

*Sometimes I feel so young*
*and unequipped.*
*Give me confidence*
*in my God-given abilities*
*and help me to trust*
*that you have placed me*
*on exactly the right path.*

*When I feel conflicted*
*between my own ambitions*
*and what you are calling me to do,*
*I pray you will bring peace*
*and clarity.*

*Father,*
*open the doors*
*you wish me to walk through*
*and close the ones you don't.*

*Amen*

*Lord,*
*I am here.*
*Speak to me.*

*I am here, Lord,*
*Tell me what you want of me.*
*I am listening.*

*You have given me skills and passions which*
*make me unique!*
*How do I use them for you, Lord?*

*You have made a plan for me,*
*Tell me where you want me to go, Lord.*

*Thank you for all you have done for me.*
*What can I do for you, Lord?*

*Give me the strength*
*to do what you made me to do.*
*I am yours, Lord.*

*Amen*

# 7 CELEBRATING ME

For it was you who formed my inward parts; you knit me together in my mother's womb.

Psalm 139:14

*Lord God,*
*thank you for making me just the way you*
*wanted me to be!*
*Thank you that you made me different from*
*anyone else.*
*A special edition!*

*You gave me talents and gifts.*
*You give me passions and dreams.*
*You lay opportunities in front of me*
*and you created me to go and live the amazing*
*plan*
*you made for me.*

*Please help me to realise*
*I am your masterpiece!*
*When I am faced with negativity*
*or voices telling me I'm not enough,*
*I pray you will remind me of my worth and beauty.*

*Amen*

---

*Lord,*
*I just wanted to take some time*
*to say thank you for creating me to be exactly the way I am:*
*completely one-of-a-kind!*

*Thank you for my* BODY*!*
*I thank you that every single part of it is perfectly and intentionally made by you,*
*from each essential organ*
*to every freckle and mole!*

*I am so grateful*
*for everything my body allows me to do.*
*I can run through beautiful fields and swim in the sea!*
*I can enjoy good food*
*and smile, speak and sing!*
*I can jump and dance in worship*
*and listen to others.*
*I can laugh with my friends,*

*hug and high-five!*

*Thank you for the colour of my skin,*
*the shade of my eyes*
*and all of my little family traits!*

*It is so incredible how quickly my body*
*can heal*
*when I get hurt*
*and that it holds absolutely everything I need*
*to be alive inside of it!*

*Thank you for my MIND!*
*God, thank you for my ability to think of new*
*ideas,*
*wonder about the world,*
*discover and dream!*
*Thank you for my mind,*
*which tells my body everything it needs*
*and can figure things out!*
*Thank you for my imagination,*
*creativity*
*and memory.*
*My mind can digest and hold so much*
*information!*
*How can one tiny brain do so much?!*

*Thank you for my SOUL!*
*I thank you for all of the things that make*
*me, ME!*
*Thank you that I enjoy laughter, friendliness*
*and kindness!*

*I have empathy towards others,*
*I can feel sad with them*
*and happy for them*
*and everything in between!*
*I am quirky, unique and passionate.*

*Lord,*
*sometimes it can be easy to forget all of these amazing things.*
*I don't always look after myself properly.*
*I pray you will help me to prioritise the things that I need,*
*to stay motivated,*
*happy and healthy!*

*Amen*

# 8 CHANGE

I am about to do a new thing; now it springs forth, do you not perceive it?

I will make a way in the wilderness and rivers in the desert.

Isaiah 43:19

*Wow, okay,*
*so I'm about to start something new.*
*And I'm terrified!*

*I know it's exciting, Lord, but I can't help but*
*think up all the things that could go*
*wrong.*
*I pray for your peace and guidance*
*as I navigate this change.*

*Amen.*

*Lord,*
*I'm excited for the future.*
*I have dreams!*
*I can do what I love!*
*I won't be forced to go to school each day to study things I don't care about.*
*I want to grow.*
*I want to change,*
*to become more confident,*
*to discover new skills,*
*but, I'm also afraid.*

*My life right now is what I'm used to.*
*I know my way around,*
*I know the people who are around me each day.*
*I'm worried I'll wish for all this back.*
*I mean, it sounds scary,*
*suddenly being surrounded by new people,*
*new areas,*
*having to be more independent.*

*I will feel so lost.*
*My expectations are so high for the future,*
*But what if everything goes horribly?*
*I wish everything would be so clear.*

*God, you made a plan for me,*
*So why can't you just tell me?*
*It would make me feel so much more calm*

*and it would make decisions so much easier!*

*Help me not to wish my life away,*
*but appreciate every moment.*
*Keep me positive and trusting in you,*
*always.*

*Amen*

# 9 CHURCH

For where two or three are gathered in my name, I am there among them.

Matthew 18:20

*Church is GREAT!*
*I LOVE it!*
*What an incredible thing that we can praise you FREELY!*
*THANK YOU!*
*Amen*

*Lord,*
*what is church all about?*
*Sometimes I find it all a bit weird.*
*I just go along*

*without understanding.*
*Give me opportunities*
*to engage with it more.*
*Help me make it more about you*
*than it is me.*

*Amen*

# 10 CLIMATE CHANGE

The earth is the Lord's and all that is in it, the world, and those who live in it.
Psalm 24:1

*Dear God, we need you.*
*We need your help.*
*The beautiful planet you made for us is being destroyed.*

*Lord, I'm worried,*
*worried for my own and everyone else's future.*
*So many dreams at risk.*
*Everyone has aspirations,*
*but none of them can be achieved until we tackle climate change.*

*Everyone is blaming each other,*
*spreading hate, criticising each other,*
*when we should be working together.*

*Lord, are you angry at us?*
*It's hard to trust leaders now.*
*It's hard to know whether they want to help*
*or if they just want to look good.*

*Lord,*
*I pray for those who are making a difference.*
*For those who lead protests,*
*those who inspire and motivate,*
*those who are known,*
*and those who make small contributions*
*to help our planet.*
*Give these people the strength to keep going.*
*I pray they will continue to use the passion*
*inside of them to keep going.*

*Sometimes it feels*
*like I can't do much to help,*
*but Lord,*
*I pray you will support me*
*making small changes.*
*Please guide me*
*and make it easier to make those choices.*

*Amen*

*I don't know what to say, God.*
*The world is a mess.*
*Your creation is broken, melting and dying.*

*I want to help.*
*I want to stop the damage that is being done.*
*But I feel so small and overwhelmed,*
*hopeless and helpless.*
*Where would I begin?*

*The Bible says that through you God, I can do all things.*
*Help me remember this and find strength in you.*

*I pray that you would spark in me a passion and calling to protect the environment that is so much bigger than the discouragement and fear I feel right now.*
*Equip and embolden me.*
*When I put my trust in you Lord, I can make a difference.*
*I want to start now.*

*Amen*

# 11 COURAGE

---

"I hereby command you: Be strong and courageous; do not be frightened or dismayed, for the LORD your God is with you wherever you go."

Joshua 1:9

---

*Being courageous is hard, God.*
*I want to do the right thing,*
*but I know that this option isn't going to be easy.*
*I need to feel confident that this really is the best choice, and even though it might be difficult at first, it is all part of your amazing plan for my life.*

*Give me bravery and self-belief*
*as I approach this.*
*I am putting my total trust in you, Lord.*

*I pray for perseverance when I want to give*
*up and for your godly wisdom when I feel*
*unequipped.*
*May you give me kind, fair words in tricky*
*conversations and a deep sense of calm*
*when I feel conflicted.*

*Sometimes I feel misunderstood by other*
*people*
*and find myself constantly justifying my*
*choices to them.*
*Give me the courage to stand firm in the*
*knowledge that you use all things for good*
*and to know that when I listen to and*
*follow you,*
*everything will be okay.*

*You are a wonderful Father*
*who is always watching over and protecting*
*me.*
*Thank you that you can make me brave.*

*Amen*

---

*Lord,*
*give me courage,*
*help me to stay strong.*
*I feel weak inside*
*and you know why.*
*You know my heart so well.*

*Give me the words to speak*
*and the ears to listen*
*and the bravery to act.*
*Give me the wisdom to keep coming back*
*to you,*
*to keep building everything from you.*
*You, Lord, are my rock.*
*Thank you for staying by my side.*

*Amen*

# 12 DECISIONS

Trust in the Lord with all your heart, and do not rely on your own insight.

In all your ways acknowledge him, and he will make straight your paths.

Proverbs 3:5-6

*Decisions, decisions, decisions.*
*So many decisions!*

*Small decisions . . .*
*What should I have for tea?*
*Can I be bothered to tidy my room now?*

*Big decisions . . .*
*What GCSEs should I choose?*
*Which university should I go to?*
*What job do I want to do?*

*Life is full of decisions, God.*
*Help me to know which paths to take*
*and give me courage to trust in you*
*and your plan.*

*Amen*

---

*Gahhhh!*
*I really don't know what to do, God!*
*I have this huge decision to make*
*and it feels so out of my control.*

*It's like a massive weight pressing down*
*on me,*
*which is getting heavier the closer I get to*
*when I need to have decided.*
*I can't hold it much longer.*

*I feel like this is the biggest decision I have*
*ever made*
*and I worry that I will make*
*a terrible mistake.*

*I feel so overwhelmed,*
*I can't even identify the options to decide.*
*What if I regret it?*

*God,*
*I have made some bad choices before*
*and I am scared that this will just be another*

*one.*
*I think that these previous mistakes are holding me back*
*and making me question everything.*

*I want my decision to be full of you.*
*I pray for clear signs*
*to help me figure out what to do and what is right.*
*I want to feel happy and confident with the outcome.*

*Forgive me for when I have ignored you, Lord,*
*and pursued the things I wanted,*
*even if I knew they weren't really the right ones.*
*You have given me so much already.*

*When I look back on my life,*
*I can see you have blessed me immensely.*
*Even things I thought I wanted in the past that didn't happen,*
*I can now see why that was the case*
*and I am so grateful for it.*

*I know, that ultimately,*
*you use everything for your good.*
*Be with me in this decision and the outcome, God.*

*Amen*

# 13 DISAPPOINTMENT

For surely I know the plans I have for you, says the Lord, plans for your welfare and not for harm, to give you a future with hope.

Jeremiah 29:11

*I can't believe this has happened, Lord!*
*I feel so disappointed*
*because this really wasn't the way*
*I was hoping*
*things would turn out.*

*I know that you have a plan for me*
*and you use all things*
*for good,*
*but when I am feeling so discouraged*
*it is hard to hold on to this belief.*

*I pray that you would help me*
*to stand firm in the truth*
*that you know exactly what you're doing*
*and this is completely where I am meant*
*to be.*

*God,*
*I want to trust in you even when something*
*turns out differently*
*to how I had expected.*

*Amen*

---

*Lord,*
*everything was going so well.*
*I was happy, excited.*
*It was so perfect.*
*But now this.*

*Things have not gone as I expected.*
*This isn't how things are meant to be.*

*God,*
*you're meant to have a plan for me,*
*but I honestly can't see where this is going.*
*I want to be patient,*
*to trust,*
*but I can't stop thinking everything would be*
*so much better*
*if things had gone the way I wanted.*

*I pray you will help me to accept the way*
*things have turned out.*
*I guess not everything can always go my way,*
*but bring me peace*
*and give me the strength*
*to keep going*
*even though I feel like giving up.*

*Amen*

# 14 EVANGELISM

---

And Jesus came and said to them, "All authority in heaven and on earth has been given to me. Go therefore and make disciples of all nations, baptizing them in the name of the Father and of the Son and of the Holy Spirit, and teaching them to obey everything that I have commanded you. And remember, I am with you always, to the end of the age."

Matthew 28:18-20

---

*Hi God,*
*I want to talk to you about something.*
*You told me to go and tell people about you.*
*You mean so much to me, you make me so happy*
*and you support me when I'm struggling,*
*so why do I find it so hard*

*to talk to other people about you?*

*I think I'm scared of being judged.*
*There are so many trends and pressures*
*it feels like if I don't fit in.*
*When I start telling others how amazing*
*you are,*
*I'm worried they might not really understand*
*where I'm coming from.*
*It feels like such a risk.*

*Maybe they will ask questions*
*and want to know more.*
*Maybe they will just ignore me.*
*But what if they think*
*the whole thing is just a joke?*

*You have promised you will stay with me.*
*I pray you will just let the right words*
*flow out of me.*
*Help me not to be discouraged*
*by anything or anyone*
*and let me feel your presence.*

*Please help me not to force anything onto*
*anyone,*
*but just share with them your love with*
*passion.*
*I pray you will bring me confidence*
*and not let me feel held back by people.*

*Amen*

*I think now is a good time to tell this person*
*about you, God.*
*I pray for your courage*
*and strength*
*and that you would give me the words*
*when mine don't feel like enough.*
*I want to feel unashamed*
*as I share my faith with them.*
*May your love,*
*peace*
*and wisdom*
*shine through in what I am about to say.*

*Amen*

# 15 EXAMS

Whatever your task, put yourselves into it, as done for the Lord and not for your masters, since you know that from the Lord you will receive the inheritance as your reward; you serve the Lord Christ.

Colossians 3:23-24

*Hi God!*
*Exams can be really stressful*
*so please can you be with me*
*and help me feel calm.*

*There is so much work*
*and pressure*
*that goes into one exam.*
*Please can you make sure it doesn't weigh me down?*

*Thank you that you have a plan for me*
*and that whatever my results are*
*you will use them to make good come from it.*

*You're an awesome dad*
*who encourages me*
*and wants me to do well!*
*I know you will never be disappointed*
*with me.*

*Help me not to compare my results with those*
*of others.*
*It can make me feel bad about myself when*
*people do better than me,*
*but you are the one who made plans for me*
*and who gives me purpose.*

*Help me to remember*
*that you are my refuge.*
*You are always with me*
*and I can trust you*
*because you are the one who defines me,*
*not my results.*

*Amen*

---

*Jesus,*
*I've got some exams coming up*
*and they are making me feel pretty nervous*
*and stressed.*

*They are all I think about.*
*I feel under so much pressure from the people*
*around me to do well*
*and I don't want to let them down.*
*I don't want to feel disappointed in myself,*
*either!*

*My teachers tell me that these grades will*
*define what I can do for the rest of my life!*
*Is that really true, Lord?*
*That makes me feel even more scared,*
*but I feel like I'm the only one who feels*
*this way.*
*All of my friends seem so relaxed about our*
*exams,*
*but then again they are all so smart and I*
*know they are going to ace them!*

*This makes me feel jealous sometimes,*
*or really stupid and like I care too much about*
*succeeding.*
*I have worked really hard towards the tests,*
*so I want them to go well and reflect the best*
*of my ability.*

*I pray you will take away my fear and*
*worry, God.*
*Give me motivation*
*to continue preparing for my exams*
*and clarity of mind for when I am sitting*
*them.*
*Help me to trust in you*

*and to remember that you have a plan for me*
*and my life.*
*I know that my results don't define me*
*and that you have a wonderful plan for my*
*life regardless.*

*I pray you will help me remember this and*
*not to compare myself with others.*
*I want to celebrate their successes and*
*support them when they are disappointed.*
*I don't want to take comfort in other people's*
*inabilities,*
*which sometimes I do.*

*I thank you that you love me no matter what.*

*Amen*

# 16 FEELING FAR FROM GOD

---

Draw near to God, and he will draw near to you
James 4:8

---

*Where are you, God?*
*I have been struggling with things recently*
*and I feel like you're not around.*
*I know that I probably don't make enough*
*time to chat to you,*
*but when I have prayed before*
*I felt like you didn't answer.*

*I desperately want to feel closer to you,*
*but I don't always know how.*
*I think I often act like you are the last resort.*
*I try and sort things out on my own first and*
*then turn to you when it doesn't go to*
*plan.*

*I'm sorry for when I forget to trust in you and*
*think that I know better!*
*I want to immediately turn to you with every*
*situation I face and remember to always*
*give thanks,*
*not just pray when I am experiencing*
*something difficult.*
*So, this is me saying to you, God,*
*that I am putting you first from now on.*
*You are my number 1!*

*Amen*

---

*God,*
*where are you?*
*I pray to you,*
*I listen for you,*
*and nothing happens.*
*All I get is silence.*

*Why does it feel like my prayers are not*
*answered?*
*Why don't I feel any guidance from you when*
*life is so hard?*
*I'm really trying to find you, God.*
*I can't see you,*
*I can't touch you.*
*It feels like I'm talking to myself.*
*Why can't I just hear a loud, booming voice*
*telling me what to do?*

*Life is so hard.*
*Faith feels so hard.*
*At the moment,*
*trying to add you to my life just feels like*
*another burden,*
*too confusing.*

*I hear about encounters other people have*
*with you and they make it sound so easy.*
*I want that!*
*Why can't I have that?*
*I won't give up, God.*
*I want to experience you.*
*Please show me something:*
*a picture,*
*a song,*
*an action,*
*anything!*

*I just want to know your presence.*
*I want to be joyful,*
*to feel excited about your love.*

*I pray I will be able to look back on this time*
*in my life and realise that although I can't*
*see you doing anything,*
*you were working behind the scenes,*
*working to give me answers better than I*
*could have imagined.*

*Please give me hope and courage*
*to keep holding onto you.*

*Give me the strength to keep going*
*even when it feels like you aren't there.*
*When I feel ready to give up,*
*fill me with determination.*

*God, I reach out to you.*
*Please hold me in your arms*
*and carry me through.*

*Amen*

## 17 FEELING SCARED

Do not fear, for I am with you, do not be afraid, for I am your God; I will strengthen you, I will help you, I will uphold you with my victorious right hand.

Isaiah 41: 10

*I am extremely frightened, God.*
*I can only think of everything*
*that could go wrong no matter how much I try*
*and reassure myself.*
*Give me your security and protection.*
*I want to feel courageous,*
*knowing that I am in your right hand*
*and that you go before me in all things.*
*Be with me now, Lord.*

*Amen.*

*Lord, are you there?*
*It feels like a growing knot in my stomach.*
*Everything feels out of control.*
*I feel so weak.*

*Father, please keep me safe.*
*Stay by my side.*
*I'm so scared.*
*I don't know what is going to happen,*
*but you do.*

*I pray everything will be okay,*
*just give me courage*
*to trust in you.*

*Amen.*

# 18 FORGIVENESS

Bear with one another and, if anyone has a complaint against another, forgive each other; just as the Lord has forgiven you, so you also must forgive.

Colossians 3:13

*God,*
*Forgiveness is a tricky one.*
*If I do something wrong,*
*I know that you always forgive me,*
*but sometimes I struggle to find comfort in this,*
*and I can't stop feeling ashamed,*
*especially if I have hurt someone close to me.*

*I worry that they will never forgive me,*
*but is this fear out of regret and love for this other person or is it ego-driven and*

*because I'm worried how it will affect*
*how people see me?*

*I want to be more like you, God,*
*and forgive others easily, too.*
*However, even if I accept their apology,*
*I sometimes still find myself thinking about*
*how they have hurt me*
*and I struggle not to let this change the way I*
*feel about them.*

*I pray you will help me to not let these*
*thoughts and feelings dictate the way I*
*behave towards those who have offended*
*me.*

*I want to be able to love*
*and to forgive,*
*unconditionally,*
*just as you do.*

*Lord,*
*I'm sorry for when I don't consider how the*
*things I say and do may harm other*
*people.*
*May I be quick to listen and slow to speak.*
*Thank you so much for loving me no matter*
*what.*
*You always forgive me when I am sorry and*
*show me constant kindness.*
*In your eyes I am always loved no matter*

*what I have done, and I am so grateful for*
*this.*
*Thank you for giving your life*
*so that I may always be forgiven.*

*Amen*

---

*Father,*
*it's hard to talk about these people.*
*I have been taught to love others,*
*to forgive them when they make mistakes,*
*but I'm having a hard time with it.*

*People can be really horrible sometimes*
*and it can hurt.*
*Especially when there isn't a reason.*
*Sometimes it just feels really good to let anger*
*out through grudges,*
*but that doesn't bring me peace.*

*This is hard to say,*
*but I pray for those who have wronged me.*
*Please bring them peace and whatever it is on*
*their hearts,*
*whether it's a tough past, insecurities or any*
*other scars,*
*please take them away.*

*Maybe they have realised what they have done.*

*Maybe they haven't even acknowledged it.*
*Please help me to forgive them.*
*Help me to learn and grow,*
*to be loving but not let anyone walk over me.*

*Amen*

## 19 FREEDOM

...where the spirit of the Lord is, there is freedom. 2 Corinthians 3:17

*Freedom is so beautiful!*
*Thank you, Lord,*
*that you have broken every chain*
*so I can live my life.*

*I want to sing and shout*
*and dance for you, and praise you, Lord!*
*Thank you that I can be filled with*
*excitement and celebrate your love!*

*Amen!*

*Thank you for my freedom, God.*
*Thank you that I live in a free country where I can go to church and praise you without fear.*
*I pray for those who live in places where they have very few rights and are persecuted for their faith.*
*Give them courage and protection.*

*Thank you for my freedom, God.*
*Thank you that I can express myself however I choose.*
*I can wear and do whatever I enjoy.*
*I pray for those in situations which make them feel unable to showcase their personality through the way they look and pursue the hobbies they love.*
*May they feel celebrated and free.*

*Thank you for my freedom, God.*
*Thank you that I can be totally me without feeling scared or inhibited.*
*I pray for those who feel trapped and oppressed,*
*even in their own home.*
*Give them freedom, love and joy.*
*Thank you for my freedom, God.*
*Only you have set me free!*

*Amen*

# 20 FRIENDS AND FAMILY

Love is patient; love is kind; love is not envious or boastful or arrogant or rude. It does not insist on its own way; it is not irritable or resentful; it does not rejoice in wrongdoing, but rejoices in the truth. It bears all things, believes all things, hopes all things, endures all things.

1 Corinthians 13:4-7

*Thank you so much for my friends and family,*
*God.*
*I am constantly surprised and overwhelmed*
*by their love and kindness,*
*their support and encouragement.*
*I love celebrating my successes with them and*
*they are always there for me when I am*
*finding things tough.*

*Sometimes I think I am not a very good friend.*
*I forget about significant things other people might be going through*
*and I don't stay in touch enough.*
*I want to be more outward looking and in tune with what my friends and family are experiencing,*
*just as they are with me.*
*I pray you will show me the ways I can be there for those around me*
*and help me identify those who are struggling the most.*

*Equip me to be a good listener, Lord.*
*May my judgements and the things going on in my life not prevent me from showing compassion and understanding towards others.*
*I want my friends and family to know that they can always talk to me,*
*no matter what.*

*Thank you, God,*
*that you are such an awesome father and friend.*
*I want to be more like you in the way that I care for others.*

*Amen*

*God,*
*thank you so much for my friends and family.*
*Thank you for the people who love and care*
*for me like family.*
*Thank you for those who are there for me*
*when I need them.*

*Even though sometimes I don't get on with*
*people,*
*thank you for the times we manage to forgive*
*each other.*
*Thank you for the times we make up.*

*God, please bless all my relationships.*
*I pray for family members who I don't always*
*get along with.*
*I give you any problems my family is dealing*
*with.*
*Help me to be a good friend to those who*
*need it.*

*Amen*

# 21 GIFTS

Like good stewards of the manifold grace of God, serve one another with whatever gift each of you has received.

1 Peter 4:10

*Hi God!*
*I often hear people at church talk about God-given gifts and it got me thinking . . . what are* my *God-given gifts?*

*I know people who are amazing at hearing your voice*
*or who can share their faith with others,*
*but I don't feel like I am particularly gifted in these areas.*
*How can I serve you in other ways?*

*I pray you will help me to recognise the gifts*
*you have given me and direct me to the*
*ways I can use them for your glory.*
*Prepare me to cherish and support others as*
*they follow their calling and use their*
*gifts to serve you.*

*I don't want to feel envious of other people,*
*but motivated and encouraged by them.*
*I thank you for who you have created me to be*
*and for everyone I know who are using*
*their such individual gifts to bless others.*

*Amen*

---

*Jesus,*
*thank you for blessing me with gifts,*
*for giving me purpose.*

*Thank you that I was made differently to*
*everyone else,*
*embellished with unique skills and talents.*
*I pray you will use my passions to speak*
*to me,*
*use them to benefit others,*
*weave them into the plans made for me.*
*Help me to succeed,*
*and help me to learn from mistakes.*

*Amen*

# 22 GOSSIP

*A soft answer turns away wrath, but a harsh word stirs up anger.*
*Proverbs 15:1*

*Gossip!*
*Gossip!*
*Gossip!*
*I'm surrounded by it*
*and trapped by it!*
*It's become a habit*
*and I can't seem to help but join in.*
*Sometimes it feels like it's the only way to*
*make conversation*
*and to connect with people,*
*but it leaves me feeling empty, angry*
*and not myself.*

*Lord,*
*I pray you will forgive me for all the times I have talked about others behind their backs and contributed to such negativity.*
*I know that it is not kind and not of you.*
*Help me to speak words of positivity, love and encouragement*
*even when it feels counter-cultural.*
*You are so, so good to me, Lord,*
*and I want to share this in the things that I say.*

*Amen*

---

*Father,*
*there is so much gossip.*
*It's stressful.*
*I always get drawn in if my friends are talking about other people.*
*Even if I don't want to talk behind someone's back it makes people listen to me and it feels good to be appreciated.*

*I don't want to be 'that person' who tries to ruin everyone else's fun.*
*I wish everyone would just grow up or find other things to talk about.*
*Sometimes though it's not like that.*
*Sometimes I hear something about someone else and I'm dying to learn more.*

*There is something so satisfying about*
*knowing about other people.*
*I wish it wasn't.*

*God,*
*please help me not to get distracted by other*
*people's business.*
*Gossip is painful.*
*Sure, it doesn't feel like such a bad thing*
*talking about others,*
*but when someone has been talking about me*
*it feels so different.*
*If one person thinks this about me then maybe*
*everyone does!*
*Realising not everyone likes me is so hard and*
*then knowing other people have been*
*talking about me is painful.*

*It makes me feel worthless, stupid, unloved.*
*It makes me think that everyone who has*
*spoken to me has been judging me.*
*It makes me feel paranoid that people who*
*claim to be my friends have just been*
*faking it.*

*If my friends gossip all the time,*
*how can I trust they don't gossip about me?*
*These thoughts drain my energy,*
*take away my confidence,*
*make me sad,*
*make me panic.*

*I wish everyone was less judgmental and more kind especially as we don't know each other the way you do.*

*God, please help me not to get drawn into gossip and help me not to judge others. Take away my negative thoughts.*

*Amen*

# 23 GOVERNMENT AND POLITICS

---

First of all, then, I urge that supplications, prayers, intercessions, and thanksgivings be made for everyone, for kings and all who are in high positions, so that we may lead a quiet and peaceable life in all godliness and dignity.

1 Timothy 2:1-2

---

*There's a lot going on in the world right*
*now, God.*
*A lot of decisions are being made by the*
*government and different world leaders.*
*I want to try and understand what is*
*happening,*
*but it can be really confusing.*
*I hear people complaining about politics all*
*the time which makes me feel worried.*
*Am I right to feel like this?*

*I pray that you will help those in positions of power*
*to make the right decisions.*
*May they have godly wisdom and compassion,*
*for everyone living in their country*
*as well as the planet as a whole.*

*Amen*

---

*Dear God . . .*
*Politics!*
*Some say boring, some say interesting!*
*There are so many different views and opinions.*
*I'm always hearing different politicians on the news giving speeches saying why their views are best.*
*People get so angry about it, shouting at the TV and radio!*

*I guess it's a big deal,*
*who's running our country,*
*how everything should be run.*

*It must be stressful being in charge,*
*the whole country counting on you,*
*always someone disagreeing with you,*
*and so many issues to deal with.*

*Lord,*
*I pray for all politicians.*
*Help them to do their best to help others.*
*Give them wisdom and support.*

*Amen*

# 24 GUILT

For your name's sake, O Lord, pardon my guilt, for it is great.

Psalms 25: 11

*Hi, God!*
*I'm feeling pretty guilty at the moment.*
*I made a mistake*
*and although I have sorted it all out and apologised to all the people I need to,*
*I can't seem to let go of this deep sense of remorse.*
*It is all I can think about and it is eating away at me,*
*preventing me from moving forward.*
*I feel so insecure and paranoid,*
*like everyone can see what I have done and are judging me for it.*

*God,*
*I pray for your forgiveness and peace.*
*Fill me with your Holy Spirit*
*so that I can accept the situation and go forward guilt-free.*
*I pray this in your name.*

*Amen*

---

*God,*
*there is a weight on my shoulders.*
*I have done something and now it aches my heart.*
*I feel guilty Lord.*
*I am afraid of what others think of me.*
*I wish I could go back in time and undo things,*
*but I can't.*

*God, I am sorry.*
*Please forgive me.*
*I give my sins to you,*
*make me clean, Lord.*
*I am yours.*
*Help me to start afresh.*

*Even though I will make mistakes again,*
*give me the courage and strength to keep holding onto you*
*and to live the way you want me to.*

*Saying sorry is really hard.*
*Please give me the confidence to apologise to others when I need to.*
*Give me the courage to be honest and help me to rebuild relationships.*
*Please God,*
*take away the sick feeling inside of me.*
*Take away negative feelings of the past.*
*Make me new again.*

*Lord,*
*break all the chains weighing me down*
*and plant a new joy inside of me.*
*Thank you for your eternal love.*
*Thank you that you died for me so I don't have to bear the weight of sin.*
*Thank you that I can come back to you even after I rejected you.*
*Thank you that you wait for me with your arms open.*

*Amen*

# 25 HEALING

The prayer of faith will save the sick, and the Lord will raise them up.

James 5:15

*Father God,*
*I'm praying for your healing.*
*Someone I love is unwell and I really want them to get better.*
*It is extremely hard to know that they are struggling with so much pain and anxiety*
*and so I ask that you take it all away from them.*
*I pray for your healing, comfort and peace in such a sad and difficult time.*
*Place people around them who bring joy and can help and support this person when they are feeling at their worst.*

*I pray that they will receive the best care and*
*medical treatment and feel reassured by*
*this, knowing that you are with them.*
*Seeing them suffer so much makes me feel*
*helpless.*
*Equip me to support them in any way I can.*
*Return them to their happy, strong and*
*healthy self.*

*Amen*

---

*Lord,*
*I pray for* [*insert name*].
*I pray you will heal them.*
*They need you.*
*They are suffering and you can make them*
*better.*

*God,*
*please comfort them,*
*stay by their side,*
*give them comfort.*
*Keep them positive,*
*bring them hope.*
*Keep their family calm and patient.*

*Lord,*
*I pray you will keep them safe.*

*Amen*

# 26 HOMELESSNESS

I was hungry and you gave me food, I was thirsty and you gave me something to drink, I was a stranger and you welcomed me, I was naked and you gave me clothing, I was sick and you took care of me, I was in prison and you visited me.

Matthew 25: 35-36

*God,*
*as I was walking home today,*
*I passed a lot of rough sleepers*
*and homeless people.*
*It's just so crazy to think that we still live in a world*
*where others don't have a safe,*
*restful place*
*to sleep.*

*How can there be such wealth and yet such*
*poverty?*
*I pray for those who I walked past today.*
*Please give them strength and protection.*
*May they remember their worth and know*
*how much you love them.*

*I thank you for all the charities who provide*
*shelter and support for those with*
*nowhere to call home.*
*Help them to continue their work,*
*spreading your kindness and compassion.*
*I pray for guidance in the ways that I too*
*might help those who don't have a stable*
*place to live.*

*Today, I felt guilty as I carried on walking by.*
*I felt scared to stop*
*because I was unsure what to say*
*or do to help.*
*I never want my fear to get in the way of*
*serving you again, Lord.*

*Help me to trust in you more.*
*I thank you that I have a safe and cosy place*
*to live.*
*Forgive me for when I take this for granted.*
*I pray this in Jesus' name,*

*Amen*

*God,*
*I can't stop thinking about the people on the streets.*
*It's all so hard for them:*
*not knowing when they will next have something to eat;*
*suffering in the cold at night;*
*not having people to talk to.*

*As I walk home along the streets, I see people who have no home to go to, no family waiting for them, no meal ready for them.*

*God, they all have stories.*
*They all have a past.*
*I pray over their stories and bring them to you.*
*You know them so well.*

*Please, Lord,*
*provide for them.*
*Use them.*
*Show them the love you have for them.*
*Give me courage to help them,*
*whether that's having a quick chat with them or bringing them a coffee.*

*God,*
*please support all the charities providing for them.*
*Keep them strong, Lord.*

*Amen*

## 27 JEALOUSY

---

Envy rots the bones.
Proverbs 14:30

---

*Gosh, I am feeling ridiculously jealous right now, God.*
*I feel like I am literally dripping with envy*
*and I can't seem to wash it off.*
*I constantly compare myself to others*
*and I don't know how to stop.*

*I wish I looked like them.*
*I wish I had their house and belongings.*
*I wish I lived as happily and easily as them.*
*I wish I was as funny, intelligent, kind.*

*I find myself imagining being someone completely different*

*and then feeling disappointed when I think*
*about the reality of my life,*
*even though I know I am so fortunate.*

*Being this jealous can make me feel lonely*
*and angry towards others, too.*
*I don't want to feel negatively towards my*
*friends*
*because I am envious of what they have.*
*How do I appreciate and feel satisfied with*
*me and my life?*

*I pray that you will transform this part of me*
*which is overcome with such jealousy.*
*Fill me with your joy and grace.*
*I want to feel happy with who I am and enjoy*
*everything around me,*
*celebrating my friend's achievements.*
*Take away the anger and loneliness that my*
*envy causes*
*and all of the insecurities that feed it.*
*Help me to remember that my life is part of*
*your perfect plan.*

*Amen*

---

*God, it feels like you made them perfect.*
*You gave them the perfect body,*
*you surrounded them with amazing friends,*
*you gave them talents,*

*you made them confident.*

*But what about me God?*
*Why haven't I received what I asked for?*
*I hate to say it because I know I'm meant to love everyone,*
*but this person brings me so much anger!*
*They have everything and yet they don't appreciate it.*
*I know I'm not meant to be judging others,*
*but I just can't help noticing any tiny fault when I see one.*
*I guess I'm trying to convince myself they aren't perfect.*

*Lord,*
*if I had their life*
*I believe I could never be horrible to anyone.*
*That's why they make me angry.*

*Lord, I'm sorry.*
*I know you made everyone different*
*and you love me loads,*
*but I just can't help wishing I were them.*

*Lord, it's hard to admit,*
*but I'm so jealous.*
*Help me to be happy when I see things going well for others.*
*I don't know them like you do.*
*Maybe things aren't as good for them as they seem.*

*Lord,*
*help me to be more loving,*
*help me to be more thankful*
*for what I have.*

*Amen*

# 28 LIFE AT HOME

---

If it is possible, so far as it depends on you, live peaceably with all.

Romans 12:18

---

*God,*
*being at home can be great.*
*I live in a beautiful and safe place,*
*with some amazing opportunities*
*and facilities.*
*I have a warm safe house, which I share with*
*my kind and supportive family,*
*and a bedroom which I can decorate and*
*make my own.*
*But recently I haven't been enjoying being*
*here as much.*

*Sometimes, I feel like where I live is way too small,*
*lacking things to do.*
*I feel that nobody else is my age and they don't understand.*
*I crave being in the big wide world,*
*where I can do and be anything I want.*

*Lord,*
*sometimes it feels like everyone in my family has been extra busy and so when we come back from work and school, it can feel stressful and fraught.*
*Arguments start and it is difficult to relax and enjoy being all together.*
*Sometimes I struggle to find a quiet place to do my homework*
*and I can feel overlooked and lonely.*

*I pray for peace for me and my family*
*so that our evenings together are calm and fun,*
*where we can unwind and chat.*

*I pray for more opportunities to engage with and to appreciate where I live at the moment and to know that I am exactly where I am supposed to be right now in your eyes, Lord.*

*Amen*

*Thank you for my family, Lord.*
*Thank you for all the happy memories at home.*

*Lord, I pray over my family.*
*Sometimes things are quiet at home*
*and sometimes things are loud*
*and lots of the time things are very chaotic!*

*I pray for the people who look after me.*
*They are good at coming across as strong, good at being there for me.*
*Maybe everything isn't always as it seems though.*
*I pray for my family,*
*for the issues that are out in the open and for the emotions that are locked away.*

*Lord,*
*I also pray for those who don't feel happy at home.*
*I pray for those whose families have split apart.*
*Give them strength.*

*I pray for those who feel lonely and confused.*
*Give them comfort.*
*I pray for those who don't know how loved they are.*
*I pray for those who are scared at home,*

*those who live in fear.*

*Please, God,*
*be there for them.*
*Give them courage,*
*keep them safe and give them hope*
*because things are going to get better.*

*I pray for those who feel lost in their family,*
*those who feel different,*
*as if they don't fit in.*

*I pray for those around me who feel like they*
*are suffering and can't be heard.*
*Please let them know that you are listening.*
*I pray for those with new family,*
*that they will feel settled.*

*There are so many different families, Lord.*
*Thank you that whatever our family situation*
*is, we can find a home in you always.*

*Amen*

# 29 LONELINESS

Where can I go from your spirit?
Or where can I flee from your presence?
If I ascend to heaven, you are there;
if I make my bed in Sheol, you are there.
If I take the wings of the morning
and settle at the farthest limits of the sea,
even there your hand shall lead me,
and your right hand shall hold me fast.
Psalm 139:7-10

*I feel so alone, God.*
*Alone in bustling public places.*
*Alone when I am at home with all my family.*
*Even when I've been out with my friends, I come home and feel overwhelmingly isolated.*

*I feel different and separate from everyone*
*else and I don't know why.*
*I want to feel happy and care-free,*
*fully engaged with the loving people that*
*surround and support me.*
*I want to feel a sense of purpose and*
*enthusiastic about something!*

*At the moment,*
*I just feel bored and tired.*
*I want to shut myself in my bedroom and*
*never come out,*
*but then I know this would make me feel even*
*more on my own.*

*I pray you will reach to me in my loneliness,*
*Lord,*
*and pull me out of it.*
*Give me more opportunities to meet like-*
*minded people who are the same age*
*as me.*
*I pray for welcoming places and people who I*
*can connect with and really enjoy*
*hanging out with.*
*I don't want to feel alone anymore.*

*Father,*
*I thank you that you are always with me.*

*Amen*

*Lord, there are so many people around me*
*and yet I'm lonely.*
*I have friends, but no one really close,*
*no one who really gets me.*

*God, are you there?*
*I know you are there.*
*I know you know me*
*and love me*
*and that I can talk to you about anything,*
*but I don't always feel like this is a friendship.*
*I can't phone or text you and get a clear reply.*

*God,*
*help me to connect with people who love me,*
*and who want to listen to me.*

*Amen*

# 30 LOSS

For I, the Lord your God, hold your right hand; it is I who say to you, 'Do not fear, I will help you.'
Isaiah 41:13

*I need you right now, God,*
*more than I think I ever have.*

*I feel like I have a huge hole right through my chest,*
*hollow and empty.*
*It hurts to breathe and I feel saturated with sadness.*
*I feel deflated and like I am trapped in some horrible dream.*

*Has this really just happened?*
*I genuinely can't picture what life will look*

*like from now and this absolutely terrifies me.*
*I can't walk any further right now, God.*
*I need you to carry me through this loss.*
*I pray for your strength, healing and joy, God.*

*Get me through the painful time I'm in.*

*Amen*

---

*Father,*
*this is your child speaking.*
*I'm grieving.*
*I have so much going on in my head right now.*
*I feel so broken,*
*so sad,*
*angry even.*

*Lord, I need you.*
*I don't know why I have to be going through this.*
*I don't understand, I don't know how to cope.*
*I feel like I'm expected to stay strong for the sake of everyone else.*
*I just want to be sad.*
*It almost feels wrong to smile.*
*I don't want to be happy.*
*I need to cry.*
*I feel so weak and I just want to mourn.*

*I feel regret,*
*if only I knew this was going to happen,*
*I wish I had valued every moment with them more.*

*Father, I need you!*
*Father, I cry to you!*

*I'm so tired.*
*I don't know how I can find strength to keep going.*
*I don't feel like smiling,*
*I don't feel like talking to friends.*

*I have changed.*
*Everything is so different.*
*Show me where to go.*
*Motivate me.*
*Tell me everything is going to be okay.*
*This weight is too heavy to carry alone.*
*Show me that you never let me walk alone.*
*Show me you are with me , Lord.*

*Father, this isn't how things will be forever is it?*
*I don't want to feel trapped in grief forever.*
*It's hard to see that I could be happy again.*
*I just need you to comfort me, Father.*
*Please bring me peace.*
*Bring my family peace, Lord.*

*Amen*

# 31 MAKING FRIENDS

---

For I am convinced that neither death, nor life, nor angels, nor rulers, nor things present, nor things to come, nor powers, nor height, nor depth, nor anything else in all creation, will be able to separate us from the love of God in Christ Jesus our Lord.

Romans 8:38-39

---

*Hi God!*
*I'm about to start something new and I'm*
*worried I will struggle to make friends.*
*I'm scared I'll be really different to everyone*
*else,*
*especially because of my faith.*
*I want to find people who I can enjoy being*
*myself around*
*and not feel I have to compromise who I am*
*just to fit in.*

*I would love to have a group of really good long-term friends,*
*where we can all support each other as we face challenges in life.*
*I pray you will place friends there for me who I will instantly connect and have a laugh with.*
*May they be fun, encouraging and bring out the best in me.*

*Thank you for every kind of friendship, God.*
*Fun ones,*
*short ones,*
*long-distance or for-life ones.*

*Equip me to make friends easily.*
*I pray you will give me clarity and space to notice those who might be feeling lonely and left out,*
*and kind words to make them feel welcome.*
*I want to be like the approachable, caring friends I hope to make.*

*Help us to be thoughtful and empathetic listeners,*
*so that we can all be there for each other*
*during this time of change.*

*Amen*

*God,*
*I'm nervous about something.*
*I keep seeing friendship groups.*
*Groups where everyone gets along,*
*everyone loves each other,*
*supports each other*
*and want to be with each other*
*all the time.*

*God, I really want that.*
*I really want close friends.*
*It just seems so hard,*
*all the starting conversation and the getting to know each other.*
*I don't feel confident.*

*God,*
*please bring me the friends I need.*
*Bring people into my life who I will click with.*

*Help me to not be discouraged*
*and to keep holding onto you.*

*Amen*

# 32 MISSING OUT

And my God will fully satisfy every need of yours according to his riches in glory in Christ Jesus.
Philippians 4:19

*Feeling like you are missing out*
*can be scary, God.*
*When you are doing something different to*
*most other people your age,*
*it can be easy to feel like you aren't*
*experiencing the same exciting*
*opportunities as them.*

*Sometimes I wish I was involved in things I*
*am not particularly interested in just in*
*case I will feel left out or like I might not*
*be having as much fun as my friends . . .*
*sports-teams, parties, classes at school.*

*I want to feel content with where I am in my*
*life and the choices I make,*
*not rejected and lonely.*

*When I see posts on social media*
*of what other people have been doing,*
*it makes me feel boring*
*or disliked.*
*"Surely, there must be a reason I wasn't*
*invited?"*

*I pray you will take away this cycle of*
*comparison and negativity,*
*replacing it with joy and thanks*
*for everything you have given to me.*

*Surround me with opportunities and*
*friendships*
*which allow me to feel included and*
*enlivened,*
*spaces where I can enjoy being myself*
*and doing the things I love.*

*Lord,*
*help me to remember that everything has a*
*season,*
*and I am exactly where you want me to be.*

*Amen*

*Lord,*
*why am I not happy?*
*My life isn't bad.*
*I guess just seeing everyone together,*
*laughing,*
*loving,*
*partying.*
*People always texting,*
*hanging out,*
*talking.*
*I just always have this fear of missing out.*
*I'm worried I'm doing something wrong.*

*Sometimes I feel different.*
*I haven't watched the film everyone is talking about.*
*I didn't go to that party everyone was invited to.*

*Lord,*
*help me to remember that I'm probably not the only one to worry like this.*
*Help me to reach out to others.*

*Amen*

# 33 NEWS

The light of the eyes rejoices the heart, and good news refreshes the body.

Proverbs 15:30

*Woohoo!*
*Good news!*
*Thank you, thank you, THANK YOU, God,*
*for such GOOD news!*

*Your love is immense and your blessings are*
*unimaginable.*
*When I feel deflated and lost,*
*you give me hope and joy.*
*I shout my praise to you!*
*Yay!*
*Amazing news!*

*Thank you, thank you, THANK YOU God*
*for such AMAZING news!*

*Your kindness is breathtaking and your power*
*is miraculous.*
*When I feel like everything is so much bigger*
*than me,*
*you give me strength and peace.*
*I shout my praise to you!*

*Wow!*
*Wonderful news!*

*I just can't believe such WONDERFUL*
*news!*
*I THANK YOU God for your constant*
*generosity.*

*I shout ALL of my praises to you!*

*Amen*

---

*Lord,*
*hearing the news can make me feel upset.*
*I'm just constantly hearing about death,*
*wars,*
*crimes and suffering.*

*Our world is so full of negativity*
*and I forget the positive things.*

*The worst thing is when I feel like there isn't*
*much I can do.*
*I don't understand why some people have it so*
*hard and yet I have so much.*

*Help me to appreciate what I have, Lord.*
*I pray that you will be with people who are*
*struggling and let them know your*
*presence.*
*You hear every prayer, God.*
*Please give them strength and courage to face*
*the future,*
*for you are a firm foundation*
*and only with your help can we make the*
*world peaceful.*

*Help me to make a difference*
*even when I know some things are beyond my*
*power.*

*Amen*

# 34 POVERTY

The Spirit of the Lord is upon me, because he has anointed me to bring good news to the poor.

Luke 4:18

*God,*
*Recently I have been thinking about poverty*
*and all of the people in the world who are*
*not as fortunate or privileged as I am.*
*There are so many people who don't have the*
*basic things to survive and live*
*comfortably . . .*
*a home,*
*clothes,*
*food,*
*money,*
*work and education . . .*
*all the things I take for granted.*

*Every day others are risking their lives to feed
their families and send their children to
school,
whereas I have never had to think about
where my next meal will come from.
There are people living in areas of such
conflict and devastation,
who are constantly scared and vulnerable.*

*We complain about politics and our
government,
but we are so lucky to live somewhere safe
and peaceful,
where our voices are heard.*

*I ask for your love and justice to flood into
these areas of poverty and violence.
Protect and embolden those who are
defenseless and oppressed.
Bring hope and joy to those who struggle
every day just to survive.*

*Thank you for all the amazing organisations
that provide aid to those facing extreme
poverty.
I pray that they will continue to provide such
life-changing support around the world,
and bring about a dramatic change which
will demolish poverty and bring total
equality.
I pray for all of the people who are subject to
poverty in my own community.*

*May there be an abundance of people they can turn to for help.*

*Forgive me, God, for not always recognising how privileged I am*
*and for all of the things I forget to say thank you for.*
*I want to do everything I can to strive towards a world full of you, Lord.*
*Equip me to serve you and those living in poverty in any way I can.*

*Amen*

---

*Lord,*
*it's heartbreaking to see people on the street,*
*hungry, and lonely.*
*It's terrible seeing families on television who have to work so hard to keep alive, struggling, starving.*

*It makes me realise how lucky I really am.*
*God, why are you letting them live like this?*
*God, I want to help. Show me what to do.*
*You love these people.*

*I pray for those working to support people who live in poverty.*
*Give them strength each day.*
*Keep inspiring them*

*and keep motivating them.*

*Work through them, Lord.*
*Thank you for the work they do.*
*I ask that you will help us all to keep making*
*a difference.*

*God, please, no problem is beyond you.*
*Help us, Lord!*
*Help us to tackle poverty.*

*Amen*

# 35 PRAYER

Whatever you ask for in prayer with faith, you will receive.

Matthew 21:22

*Hi God!*
*Sometimes,*
*I struggle to chat to you.*
*Give me quiet*
*when I can't seem to find the time or space for you.*
*Give me words*
*when mine don't seem*
*quite enough.*

*Amen.*

*God, help me to focus.*
*Take away all the distractions.*
*I'm finding prayer difficult.*
*I hear prayers that are so fancy and long and*
*make no sense to me.*
*I just want to talk to you; that's what prayer is*
*isn't it?*
*But it's not like talking to another person.*
*It feels different, harder.*

*How do I know you are listening?*
*Why don't I hear you say something back?*
*It would be so much easier if I could see you.*
*How do I talk to someone I can't see?*
*How do I have a relationship with someone I*
*can't touch, can't hear?*

*Sometimes I feel like I am talking to myself*
*but just slip in "dear God" as I start.*
*Is that still prayer?*
*What if my prayer isn't answered?*
*I just need to be patient and trust you are*
*already sorting things.*
*I want to feel like I'm having a conversation.*

*God,*
*please talk to me, help me to learn your voice.*
*Please help me to know your presence,*
*And help me to know you're listening.*
*Show me the power of prayer.*

*Amen*

# 36 SCHOOL

---

Blessed are those who trust in the Lord, whose trust is the Lord. They shall be like a tree planted by water, sending out its roots by the stream. It shall not fear when heat comes, and its leaves shall stay green; in the year of drought it is not anxious, and it does not cease to bear fruit.

Jeremiah 17: 7-9

---

*God,*
*I hate school.*
*It's stressful.*
*So much pressure,*
*too many exams.*
*So many people,*
*too many trends,*
*So many opinions of who I should be,*
*how I should behave,*

*who I should be around,*
*what I should wear.*
*And do.*

*I feel like I don't fit in.*

*I know that I am so lucky to be able to go to school and I don't want to feel all these horrible feelings towards it.*
*Please help me to remember the blessing that it is.*
*Help me use the gifts you have given me to thrive in school and enjoy it.*
*Be with me when I feel worried in the classroom and overwhelmed in the corridors.*
*Surround me with people who I can be myself around,*
*who support me and love me.*
*Help me to look out for others who might also be finding it tricky so that I can be an encouragement and friend to them.*
*I pray you will help me to notice the little things to brighten up my day when I'm finding it tough.*
*I thank you that you are always with me, God,*
*and I pray that you will help me to always remember this.*

*I want to feel comfortable and confident in school today,*
*uninhibited and completely myself.*

*Thank you that I have this incredible*
*opportunity to learn so much about the*
*amazing world you created*
*and to develop some of the gifts and skills you*
*have blessed me with.*

*God,*
*thank you that I can do all things*
*when I put my trust in you.*

*Amen*

---

*Lord,*
*it feels like there are so many rules!*
*Rules about how I must I act,*
*rules about what I say,*
*even rules about the way I look.*

*It's like there is this image, this impossible*
*image I have to live up to,*
*and if I don't, then I'm not good enough.*

*School is an amazing place where I can learn,*
*where I can meet new people,*
*make new friends and have fun so I*
*thank you!*
*It can be really positive.*
*But it can sometimes feel like a really*
*negative environment.*
*It can feel like I am constantly being judged.*

*Judged through exams, how quickly I learn*
*things.*
*Judged through my interests.*
*Judged through who I hang out with.*
*Judged through what I look like.*
*It's like everything I do is being judged!*
*I start trying to become who other people*
*want me to become and, God, I know I*
*shouldn't be trying to become someone*
*that I'm not!*

*Please help me become the person you called*
*me to be.*
*When I feel rejected,*
*help me to remember that I'm accepted*
*by you.*
*When I feel I should look different to how*
*I do,*
*remind me that I was made by a wonderful*
*creator who never makes mistakes.*

*I pray you will break this cage of insecurity*
*and help me to grow my confidence.*
*Whenever I feel stressed or anxious*
*help me to cast all my anxiety on you.*
*Thank you that you love me no matter what.*
*Your love is unconditional.*
*School can be tough,*
*but I pray you will walk alongside me and*
*when it is hard, give me strength.*

*Amen*

# 37 SUCCESS

...whatever you do, in word or deed, do everything in the name of the Lord Jesus, giving thanks to God the Father through him.

Colossians 3: 17

*Wow, I was not expecting this God!*
*Thank you!*
*I have worked really hard for this and I am so pleased and proud of myself that it paid off!*
*Thank you for my gifts*
*and for such an incredible opportunity.*
*Help me to remember*
*my worth and success*
*when I think my ability isn't enough*
*and to know that this achievement*
*is amazing,*

*but it doesn't completely define me.*
*I want my successes to serve you, Lord.*

*Amen*

---

*Good qualifications, a good job, earning lots of money . . .*
*Lord, it feels like I will only be a success if I have all these things!*
*It feels like if I don't get good grades in school,*
*if I don't do as well as the people around me,*
*I won't get a good job, and I will be a failure.*

*There is so much pressure put on following in people's footsteps*
*or making sure every second counts towards achieving these things and becoming a 'success'.*
*Why am I not good enough?*
*Will I be happy once I've made everyone else proud?*

*Lord, what if I let everyone down?*
*Will you still be proud of me?*
*Sometimes it feels like I have to please everyone around me to be successful,*
*but help me to build my foundations on you,*
*and no one else.*

*Amen*

# 38 SUFFERING

He will wipe every tear from their eyes.
Death will be no more;
mourning and crying and pain will be no more,
for the first things have passed away.
Revelation 21:4

*Drought!*
*Famine!*
*Flooding!*
*Terrorism!*
*Deforestation!*
*War!*

*And that's just a few of the news headlines*
*from today, God.*
*How is it that I live in a warm, safe house,*
*with food to eat,*

*while others are hungry and vulnerable?*

*I pray for those all over the world who are not*
*as privileged as me.*
*May there be safety and peace for those living*
*in areas torn up by conflict and hatred.*
*For places inflicted with disease and*
*starvation, I ask that you bring healing*
*and provision, Lord.*

*Sometimes I battle with being positive and*
*praising you*
*when there is so much pain and suffering in*
*the world.*
*Other times, I feel like I hear the news and*
*think about how awful it is,*
*but then quickly forget about it whilst I carry*
*on my day without doing anything to help*
*those in need.*

*God, equip me to help and serve others as*
*Jesus did.*
*I want to support and care for those who are*
*struggling in my own community.*
*I pray that you will help me identify who*
*these people are and what I can do to*
*help.*

*Amen*

*God,*
*when I think about the suffering in the world,*
*I feel so sad.*
*It feels like if one more thing goes wrong,*
*I'm going to lose it.*
*The world is so big*
*and I feel so small and insignificant in it.*
*I want everything to be okay.*
*Please make it right.*

*Amen*

# 39 THANKS

O give thanks to the Lord, for he is good; for his steadfast love endures forever.

1 Chronicles 16: 34

*God, I don't say thank you enough.*
*When I chat to you it is usually just to ask for help with something and I forget to recognise and praise you for everything you have done for me!*
*Everyday I am mesmerized by your creation and how you have placed me in such a safe and beautiful home.*
*You have surrounded me with so many fun, loving and encouraging people who build me up and cherish me for who I am, but who aren't afraid to call me out when I make mistakes.*

*I am able to go to school, church and clubs without feeling afraid and you have given me so many special skills and talents I can use to help others and to serve you.*

*I thank you that you are always with me and hear every prayer.*
*You carry me through tough times.*
*You sprinkle each day with tiny blessings.*
*Thank you for your almighty strength,*
*endless kindness and humour, God.*

*Thank you that I can do anything with you!*

*Amen*

---

*Hi, God!*
*So . . .*
*I know my life isn't always perfect,*
*things make me sad or angry or jealous, and it's really nice to be able to talk to you about it but I just wanted to say thanks!*
*Thank you that I'm loved!*
*Thank you for laughter,*
*thank you for music,*
*thank you for dancing!*

*Thanks for the person who smiled at me,*
*thanks for the person who made me laugh.*

*Thanks for the big things and the little things.*
*Help me to really appreciate all the tiny details*
*you weave into my day.*
*Thank you for answers to prayer that get me so excited!*
*Thank you for that feeling when I can smell food*
*and can get excited about eating it!*
*Thank you for the days when I just feel happy for no particular reason!*
*Thank you for nature!*
*The birds,*
*the trees,*
*the flowers,*
*the sound of rivers!*

*Thank you for everything you've done for me!*

*Amen*

# 40 WONDERFULLY MADE

---

I praise you, for I am fearfully and wonderfully made.

Psalm 139:14

---

*Thank you that I was perfectly,*
*intentionally,*
*made.*

*I was made beautiful;*
*Thank you for making me strong.*

*I was made to conquer;*
*Thank you for giving me a purpose.*

*I was made to inspire;*
*Thank you for people who love me.*

*You are always with me.*
*I can do all things through Christ who*
*strengthens me.*
*Thank you that I was made*
*wonderfully me.*

*Amen*

---

*I'll be honest, God,*
*I feel pretty rubbish about myself.*
*How I look,*
*what I wear,*
*the things I say and do.*
*I feel worthless.*

*Sometimes I even think I hate myself.*
*I want to crawl out of my skin and be*
*someone, ANYONE, else.*
*Every time I go on social media I instantly*
*compare myself to other people.*
*I wish I looked like them and had their lives.*
*Even at school I don't belong.*
*I'm not as smart, confident, popular or*
*fashionable as everyone else.*
*I feel ugly, clumsy and embarrassed.*
*Why can't I just be like them?*

*I've heard people at church say everything*
*about me is intentionally and perfectly*

*created by you, so why do I still feel like this?*
*I want to feel happy and secure about the way you made me, but I don't know how to stop measuring myself against others.*
*Help me to recognise the gifts you have given me and all the amazing things about my body that you have designed.*
*I want to feel comfortable in my own skin.*

*Amen*

## 41 WRONG CROWD

Do not be deceived: Bad company ruins good morals.
1 Corinthians 15:33

*I'm not sure how I've got here, God.*
*My 'friends' aren't really my friends.*
*They say things I don't agree with and do*
*things that I don't want to do.*
*I can't keep going along with it.*
*Help me to be true to myself and what I*
*believe in,*
*to say no to things I don't agree with.*
*I pray you'll surround me with people who*
*cherish and celebrate who I am.*

*Amen*

*God,*
*I asked you for friends.*
*Friends who would love me,*
*know me,*
*care about me.*
*Friends who I could be myself around.*
*Well, I guess I have friends but they don't really feel like friends.*
*They do things that make me feel uncomfortable,*
*and say things that don't make me feel good.*
*They put me in a negative environment.*
*I guess they are nice but none of them seem to really want to know me.*
*I feel misunderstood by them.*
*Why did you let these people come into my life?*
*This wasn't what I asked you for.*
*They make me feel anxious, nervous, upset, insecure.*

*God, I want things to be different, but, God . . .*
*I'm scared of change.*
*God, encourage me to trust in you.*
*Father,*
*protect me,*
*hold me,*
*give me confidence.*

*Amen*

# About the Authors

**Martha Dommett**

Hi, I'm Martha. I'm 19 years old and I live near Bristol. At the moment, I am on a gap year and I plan to study Fine Art at University next year. I really love art and being outside, especially swimming in the sea. When I am creating something or spending time outdoors, I definitely feel closest to God. I am also really passionate about sustainability and social justice. I am so grateful to God for blessing me in so many ways and I can't wait to see what else he has in store for me!

---

**Eleanor Herbert**

Hi, I'm Eleanor. I'm 14 years old and I'm doing my first year of GCSEs right now. My favourite subjects are textiles and drama. I love doing face masks, drinking cups of tea and cooking. I find it easiest to listen to God through music and dancing! I think prayer is so important as it deepens your relationship with God and can bring so much comfort.